IP BASICS:

THE BUILDING BLOCKS FOR A SUCCESSFUL BUSINESS

(and easy mistakes to avoid along the way)

Jason H. Rosenblum, Esq.

Jacobs & Whitehall
73-03 Bell Blvd, #10
Oakland Gardens, NY 11364
www.jacobsandwhitehall.com

Ordering Information:

Quantity sales. Special discounts are available on quantity purchases by corporations, associations, and others. For details, contact the publisher at the address above.

Orders by U.S. trade bookstores and wholesalers. Please contact Jacobs & Whitehall: Tel: (888) 991-2766 or visit www.jacobsandwhitehall.com.

Printed in the United States of America

Published in 2020

ISBN: 978-1-951149-35-2

PREFACE

In your hands you have the playbook for the basic building blocks of your intellectual property ("IP"). This book is to assist you in identifying the IP in your business. Once identified the next step is deciding whether you should invest in protecting this IP. That is what this book will help you do. The basic building blocks found herein are to help you make smart decisions to capture your business's IP, retain it as an asset, and avoid infringing on another's rights.

DEDICATION

This was written during the Covid-19 crisis of 2020 and is dedicated to my isolation inmates: my wife, son, and dog. These months of self-isolation prove what I already knew. I love you more than anything and there is no one else with whom I would prefer to be isolated.

DISCLAIMER

This publication is intended to be used for educational purposes only. No legal advice is being given, and no attorney-client relationship is intended to be created by reading this material. The author assumes no liability for any errors or omissions or for how this book or its contents are used or interpreted, or for any consequences resulting directly or indirectly from the use of this book. For legal or any other advice, please consult an experienced attorney or the appropriate expert, who is aware of the specific facts of your case and is knowledgeable in the law in your jurisdiction.

Law Office of Jason H. Rosenblum, PLLC
Intellectually Protecting Your Property®
210B Rutledge Avenue
Charleston, South Carolina
(888) 666-0062
www.jhrlegal.com

TESTIMONIALS[1]

"I hired Jason Rosenblum as an attorney to assist me in obtaining 2 trademarks. My experience with Mr. Rosenblum has all been positive. He explained the entire procedure to me in layman's terms, made time to answer all of my questions, and was very patient and professional at all times. All fees are presented and explained upfront before you spend a dime. He prides himself on keeping his clients well informed throughout every stage of the process. It was very difficult for me to share my very personal ideas with someone I never met, and I felt very comfortable putting my trust in him. While Mr. Rosenblum is a terrific attorney, it is his work ethic and dedication to his client's happiness that separates him from the rest. An issue arose with another party involved in my project and Mr. Rosenblum agreed to mediate at no extra cost. He was not obligated to do so because the matter was not directly related to obtaining trademarks."

– Stephen

****

---

[1] AVVO Reviews of Jason Rosenblum
LinkedIn Reviews
Facebook Reviews
Google Maps Reviews

"Jason is an EXCELLENT lawyer. He is extremely diligent and punctual in his work, kind and determined. We go to him with all of our copyright and business questions and needs. With every copyright and title, he always gives us a time-span and stays within that time-span. Jason is on top of his work and communicates with us every step of the way. I have referred numerous colleagues of mine to him because he is the best."

– Gavin

****

"Jason has been a real asset in helping to protect the IP rights of our small businesses. He's sensitive to our cost constraints, knows what he is doing, is prompt in responding to communications, and excellent about following-up with us to get instructions when we are slow to respond (without being pushy)."

– Anonymous

****

"We've worked with Mr. Rosenblum for all of our trademark filings and he's managed the process flawlessly for over two years now. He's incredibly detail-oriented and responsive. Everyone I've referred him to is appreciative to know him. Highly recommended."

– Ken

****

"I have known and worked with Jason for the last 3 years. He is the most trustworthy and honest lawyer I have ever met. Because of this, we have become close friends. Our family values his knowledge, competency, and trust. We have recommended him to our friends."

– Al

****

"Jason Rosenblum is an amazing person, he helped me so much. He kept me updated throughout the whole process of registration and file with the state. Thank you so much, Jason. I recommend him to everyone."

– David

****

TABLE OF CONTENTS

ABOUT THE AUTHOR

I am Jason H. Rosenblum and my firm is the Law Office of Jason H. Rosenblum, PLLC. During my childhood, I was always interested in how things work. I used to take apart my toys and put them back together and loved building with Lego®. Throughout my academic career, I excelled at math and science and enjoyed physics, so when I started university, I opted for a major in mechanical engineering.

My father owned a men's clothing store and I used to work there during my college breaks. One of his customers asked if I had ever thought of going to law school and becoming a patent attorney. After that, I went home and did some research and decided to sign up for the LSAT. I started studying for it, took the test, and went to law school with the sole intention of working in patent law. However, once I started working, I found a deep interest in trademarks. That is when I started focusing most of the work that I did on trademark law, although I do patent law as well. It is from the perspective of a small business owner and lawyer that I aim to assist my clients to ensure that their IP remains an asset to their business.

What Do You Want Readers to Gain from this Book?

Over the course of my 17 years of practice, I have seen countless errors made by clients that with minimal guidance and a little bit of insight they could so easily have avoided. It is heartbreaking to see a client who has invested time, money, and effort, learn the hard way that they did something wrong and have to essentially start a project anew. When a new business or idea is in the works, the intellectual property aspect is often overlooked, but as a critical element in the value of a business, this is something I hope to encourage clients to put at the top of their to-do list.

With this book, I'm hoping not only to make small-business owners aware of the potential intellectual property pitfalls but suggest some of the best ways to sidestep costly errors and at least minimize the overall stress and expense of starting a business or brand. My ultimate ambition as a counselor to my clients is to ensure that small entrepreneurs, startups, creators, and inventors approach their intellectual property portfolio on the right foot so that it adds value to their business and so they don't have to backtrack and after years of building a brand and reputation, have to dismantle and rebuild due to a faulty foundation. I hope that readers of this book take away that, just as with every other aspect of business (i.e. marketing, accounting, bookkeeping, product development, etc.), intellectual property deserves its respect and would be best approached early on with some counseling and analysis from a lawyer with experience in the field.

CHAPTER 1

INTELLECTUAL PROPERTY (IP)

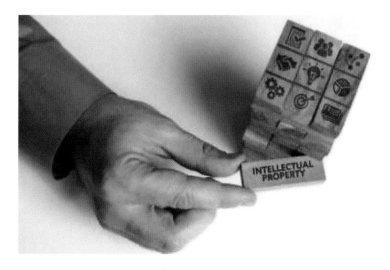

Intellectual property (IP) is an intangible asset, but as with any item of value, failure to conduct due diligence can be a costly liability. A well-known inventor Stephen Keys described intellectual property as your "perceived ownership" of an invention or an idea. By owning a copyright, a patent, a trademark, or an application for any of those, while you do have ownership over something, that thing is physically non-existent and must be otherwise claimed as your own; IP is how we claim ownership over those intangible assets.

There is no single aspect of IP protection that will guarantee your invention or creation is safe, so you need to create boundaries. There may be a number of components of IP that need to or should be addressed within one idea, product, or piece of work. Intellectual property has so many moving parts and is in constant evolution given its relationship with technology, therefore it makes sense to work with a lawyer who really understands that area of the law. An experienced attorney will help a business owner understand what they have, the value of a product it sells, what to expect when it comes time to sell the business and/or license or sell the intellectual property. Additionally, as with all things in business, there are potential risks that an IP attorney can help a business owner understand.

Areas of the Law Handled by an Intellectual Property Attorney

Intellectual property law covers patents, copyright, trademark, and trade secrets. An intellectual property attorney may handle any one of these areas or all of them. There are some intellectual property attorneys who only handle litigation of intellectual property and some who primarily work on prosecution and counseling clients about intellectual property. Prosecution of intellectual property constitutes the preparation, filing, and prosecuting of an application before the US Patent & Trademark Office or the US Copyright Office in order to obtain a registration. Litigation of intellectual property constitutes representing a client in an infringement lawsuit usually in federal court.

Areas of IP Law Handled by Our Firm

Our firm handles intellectual property law prosecution including trademarks, patents, and copyrights, as well as counseling our clients on what constitutes copyright, patent, or trademark, and how to correctly protect and defend their intellectual property. While we may send the occasional cease and desist letter or take other action if a client finds their IP being infringed upon, we may pass the matter on to a colleague or other firm for litigation if it gets to that point. There are also situations in which we need to oppose a published trademark application or at least reach out to an entity or individual who is seeking to register something too similar to a mark or brand owned by one of our clients. Ultimately, the most important part of our job is counseling a client on what intellectual property is and on how to use it to add value to and avoid liability within their business.

Clients and Industries Served by Our Firm

We work with clients in various industries. Realistically, any person or company creating a unique product, brand, composition, etc. is dealing with IP and so we have clients that range from app and software developers to fashion designers to food and beverage producers to retail shops of all sorts, to owners of coaching and consulting businesses, to various web-based companies selling products or services via the internet, and even a valve manufacturer. Our work expands outside the US to international clients as well.

When it comes to patents, often lawyers focus on a singular or specialized industry because in addition to practicing patent law well, it is immensely helpful to have familiarity with players and inventions related to that industry, however, it is not critical so long as the patent attorney is comfortable with the field of technology. For trademarks and copyrights, this is less critical of an element during prosecution and as such, an IP attorney will typically serve clients in all areas of industry.

At our firm, for patents, we primarily focus on design patents which cover the aesthetic aspects of a product, and utility patents related to mechanical and software inventions. We generally do not work with pharmaceutical, biological or plant patents, but know a number of patent attorneys well versed in those areas.

Do I Really Need an IP Attorney to Assist Me in Obtaining IP Protection?

There have been many businesses or inventors that have filed for patents, copyrights, or trademarks on their own and successfully obtained registration. But there have been more that, even if eventually successful, made mistakes that cost them dearly along the way.

Filing for trademarks and copyrights is similar to filing taxes; a lot of box-checking and fill-in the blank. But the critical part is filling in those boxes correctly to avoid making a costly mistake. And this is just the first step in the process. Even when completed correctly, an application will often meet obstacles en route to registration that will be discussed later in this book. This is why we always suggest working with a lawyer to ensure that you're taking the proper steps. We urge all business owners, inventors, creators, and entrepreneurs to at least speak with an attorney early on for a needs assessment to see if working with an attorney really is your best option. There is an old saying, "A man who is his own lawyer has a fool for a client." Even as a lawyer myself, in areas of law I am less familiar with, such as purchases and sale of real estate, drafting of wills, taxes, etc., I always use other attorneys or professionals to represent me. Separate from the legal experience that an attorney brings to the relationship, having a third-party adviser with experience in business as a sounding board adds a lot of value.

When is the Best Time to Get an Attorney Involved in an IP Plan?

It is never too early to contact an attorney regarding the plans for your IP, but it can be too late. At our firm, the initial call with a client simply covers needs assessment. We learn about the client, their situation, ask questions, and try to best understand what they have going on to figure out what options are available and help the client assess what the next step should be. Sometimes the next step is immediate action with our involvement and sometimes we suggest the client take a step back and figure out other aspects of their project and ambition before reaching out to us again in the future. Sometimes, both we and the client have homework that we need to do before proceeding or deciding what the next best action may be.

During the needs assessment conversation, we also address and assess a client's potential opportunities and the timeline within which they are looking to achieve their goals; Why do they want to act now? How soon should they take action in order to best capture those opportunities or avoid a negative consequence? What is the cost if they do or don't move forward with that opportunity? What are the potential liabilities? Who else do these decisions affect (co-owners, family, employees, managers, investors, etc.)?

In terms of patents, sometimes we see that clients just want a patent to have their name on it; some just want the monetary benefits that they believe come with owning a patent.

With both of the above examples we could simply take on these clients and file the applications for the trademark or patent, but that is not what we do at our firm. As counselors above all, our job during the needs assessment and throughout our representation is to determine whether we believe the client has a sensible plan in place that would allow them to take advantage of a registered trademark or patent and if not, to aid them in figuring one out.

If it is a patent you are seeking, we want you to have the best chance to sell the product disclosed in the patent, or have a plan to license the invention in the patent or sell the patent itself if that is what you are after. If it is glory you are after and just want to obtain and hold on to the patent for reputation then we want you to understand that the application process is an expense that most likely will not be recouped. Knowing this is your reason for applying will change our strategy. If you do not actively go out there and make something happen with the patented invention you will just spend a lot of money to get a piece of paper. If you rely on just suing infringers in hopes of winning damages, it will likely be more costly to sue infringers than the unlikely win would be worth and this is generally just not a good business model.

It can be too late to speak to or hire an attorney but never too early. If a business creates a brand and invests money in their branding, only to get a cease and desist letter because they didn't do a proper search, there is no way to backtrack and the cost to deal with litigation to hopefully fix the situation is going to be far more than it would have been to start off on the right foot.

The initial contact we have with a client or potential client is to help them gain clarity as to what their situation is. What could they do? What are the next steps? We look at their brand, product, business model, etc. and hope to come away from the meeting with better insight for both them and us, along with the best recommendations for how to proceed, whether with us right away or otherwise.

CHAPTER 2

WHAT IS A COPYRIGHT?

A copyright protects the expression of an idea when it is fixed in a tangible medium. Once you put pen to paper, save a file on your computer, or click the shutter on your camera, you're fixing your idea in a tangible medium and then, it becomes protectable.

What Does Copyright Protect?

Copyrights protect artistic works such as writings in the form of poetry, literature, books, essays, blog posts, or newsletters; photos; and musical compositions including separate copyrights for the sheet music and the actual recording of the performance of the song.

Benefits and Limitations of a Copyright

In the US, in order to sue someone for copyright infringement, you need to have an actual US copyright registration. Although a work is considered copyrighted as soon as it is fixed in a tangible medium, without registration from the US Copyright Office there is no protection of the work on a legal level and you cannot commence a lawsuit in the event that another uses and infringes on your work. Essentially if another infringes on your work and you send a cease and desist letter but do not have a registration, they most likely will ignore it since you do not have any real leverage against them to enforce your rights and obtain damages.

Having a registration before someone infringes on your copyright also means you can potentially claim your attorney's fees and can be awarded statutory damages[2] (damages award from $750 to $30,000 per work infringed) rather than having to prove the actual damages suffered which at times can be negligible or impossible to prove.

There are of course limitations to what a copyright can protect. If, for instance, a piece of art independently created was identical or similar to another, it might not be considered an infringement if it was not proven to be an intentional copy. A copyright also does not stop someone from using the information contained in a piece of work. That is, if the steps to taking an idea and turn it into a product are explained, copyright law does not stop another from using that method.

The rights in a copyright are originally owned by whomever fixes the work in a tangible medium. That is, the author of the work, the one that puts pen to paper, types on the keyboard, clicks the shutter on the

---

[2] 17 U.S. Code § 504.Remedies for infringement: Damages and profits

camera, etc. is the rightful owner. This means that if you hire or pay someone to develop your product and create your work that is the subject of a copyright you must have a work for hire agreement in place or an assignment that assigns all rights in the copyright to you, otherwise **your** work is now **their** work.

Can Anything be Registered as Copyright?

As long as it is an *original work* that falls within the definition of what is copyrightable (i.e. books, poems, plays, songs, films, sculpture, or artwork) and it is *fixed in a tangible medium*, you can file for and register a copyright.

While the base standard for a copyrightable work is apparently straightforward, some works might not meet the defined criteria. The following are not considered original copyrightable works: titles; names; short phrases; slogans; familiar symbols or designs; variations of typographic ornamentation, lettering, or coloring; and mere listings of ingredients or contents.

How Long Does a Copyright Registration Last?

If created before the 1920s, intellectual property is likely in the public domain. As a general rule, for works created after January 1, 1978, copyright protection lasts for the life of the author plus an additional 70 years. For an anonymous work, a pseudonymous work, or a work made for hire, the copyright endures for a term of 95 years from the year of its first publication or a term of 120 years from the year of its creation, whichever expires first.

Services that Our Firm Provides to Clients Looking to Obtain a Copyright

Our firm works with clients to identify their copyrightable works, sort through the different filing options based on their specific type of copyright and help them figure out what they should file for, and how to file it. We also prepare and file the copyright application to register it at the US Copyright Office. We monitor status of the application and send and receive correspondence with the Copyright Office when necessary. Upon registration, we docket the dates and advise the client of the copyright registration, the lifespan of the copyright, and answer any other questions that they might have.

Cost of Obtaining a Copyright

Our firm likes to work on flat fee rates. Generally, the cost will be somewhere between $700 and $1,000 for us to counsel, prepare, file, and monitor a single copyright application.

CHAPTER 3

WHAT IS A PATENT?

A patent is essentially a right to preclude others from practicing, making, or selling your invention. A common misunderstanding is that a patent protects an idea. This is not accurate. **Ideas** are not protectable; **inventions** are.

A patent protects inventions, and ideas lead to inventions.

For example, the idea of a flying car is not protectable, but if you invent the rockets that provide the lift for the car that could be one invention, the mechanism for steering the car could be another invention. And so on.

Protection afforded under a patent is generally much more specific than most people would expect.

What is an Invention?

An invention is any new and useful process, machine, article of manufacture, or composition of matter, or any new and useful improvement thereof.

A product like a cell phone, for example, has several patents that cover it and protect it because there are a number of inventions that allow a cell phone to work. There are patents covering the technology that enables the touch screen, the 4G and 5G technology, the ability to click on a phone number in an email and call that number, etc., as well as separate design patents that cover aesthetics of the phone including the icons on the screen, the shape of the phone, the placement of buttons, etc.

Most products have numerous potential patents that are covering all the inventions that are within the product.

Benefits and Limitations of Patents

The benefit of a patent is that it allows you to - for the length of the life of the patent[3]- stop anyone else from making, practicing, selling, and importing the invention that is claimed in the patent. Once the patent expires, however, the invention is in the public domain. That is essentially the agreement you make during your negotiations for the patent with the USPTO: you receive a limited monopoly over the invention so that others can learn from the patent and expand on it.

Another limitation is that you need to meet the statutory requirements for obtaining a patent and prove

---

[3] Currently 20 years from the earliest filing date for a utility and 15 years from issue for a design patent.

that the invention is new, useful, and non-obvious, which may be a much higher standard than you think.

Can Anything Be Patented?

For an invention to be patentable it must be of patentable subject matter, and a novel, new, useful, and non-obvious invention.

More often than not, clients come to us with an idea they think is unique, but once we start doing searches, we see that there are others who have disclosed an identical or very similar invention. In terms of "newness," if **anyone** ever disclosed your invention, anywhere, it is no longer new. They do not have to make, sell, or even patent the invention. This **anyone** includes you as the inventor. That is, if you disclose your invention in any way in a public forum (whether for sale or not) prior to applying for a patent, your patent may be barred. Disclosures prior to patenting an invention, whether in the form of another's patent, a patent application, blog post, advertisement, etc. are all considered *prior art* and if revealed in a search would prevent another too similar work from attaining a patent.

Another hurdle is obviousness. What that means is that a patent examiner can look at two or more prior disclosures and find a link that would have been obvious to a person of ordinary skill in the relevant industry to combine the teachings of those two together.

When we work with clients, one of the first and most important steps is figuring out what they believe their invention is and then, in most cases, doing a search to see what, in their invention, we think may be patentable based on the search.

The distinction between an invention and an idea is an important point we address in initial discussions with a client as well. As noted above, ideas are not patentable. Many times, clients come to us with an idea but they have not delved deeply enough into the intricacies of their invention to figure out how they actually plan to implement an idea and come up with something that is potentially patentable as an invention.

Is software patentable? These days, software has become one of the biggest concerns for most of our clients. People are creating software applications and trying to figure out what is patentable. The question is not whether the software is patentable, but whether there is an invention within the software that is patentable. Some clients develop software that has a new invention contained in the software, however, some just write new code that does not have a new inventive aspect. The law around software is currently in flux and, by nature of the software, encompasses so much that there is no clear answer as to what aspects of software are in fact patentable. Since you cannot patent a law of nature, an economic practice, or a mental process, the test is looking at a piece of software and what it does and deciding whether or not it claims or cites an abstract idea, law of nature, or natural phenomenon. If it doesn't, then there is a good chance it could be patentable or fall within subject matter patentability.

Next, we examine with as much scrutiny as possible, whether the claimed invention falls into some of the judicial exceptions that have been created. For example, if you're improving how a computer functions, that would be a patentable subject matter. Conversely, generic steps for recording, administrating, and then archiving images from a cell phone over a cellular network is probably not going to be a patentable subject matter. It is a patent attorney's job to assist their clients in determining what, if anything, falls within the patentable subject matter. With technological development being as rapid and everchanging as it is, there are new cases coming out every few months that are altering how we would counsel clients in how to proceed with inventions related to software and other related topics including business methods and processes.

Why is Conducting Due Diligence in a Search Important?

As we will discuss later in this book, ideally a business owner should do their own due diligence before investing in their invention. It is best if a business owner becomes an expert in the field in which they plan to file a patent application or disclose an invention in order to make a truly informed decision.

For patents, the due diligence we conduct on behalf of a client includes a detailed prior art search and critical assessment of the invention itself. Although it is impossible to say that with this due diligence and insight in the field, an invention will definitely lead to a patent once the application is filed, it will assist us in assessing the probability of obtaining a patent and assist us in being advocates for our clients before the USPTO. We will also be able to understand, and therefore help our clients understand, how strong their patent might be, what it will protect, what is already known in the field as general knowledge, or what is covered by another patent.

With this information and with our assistance, a client can make an educated decision as to whether the always costly patent application process is worth it now or at some point in the future.

Damages for Patent Infringement

Damages for patent infringement are governed by Patents, US Code (USC) 35, Section 284, which states that "upon finding for the claimant the court shall award the claimant damages adequate to compensate for the infringement but in no event less than a reasonable royalty for the use made of the invention by the infringer, together with interest and costs as fixed by the court." As with many rulings, this definition is somewhat vague, and the decision may be situation dependent. For example, in cases of willful infringement, damages can be enhanced to up to triple the actual amount.

Damages are generally only awarded after you receive a judgment in your favor in litigation. Calculation of the damages you may be awarded from the court and what you versus the court feels is "adequate compensation" can be at odds. This is one of the reasons our firm discourages clients from trying to obtain a patent simply in hopes of suing potential infringers as a business model.

Services that Our Firm Provides to Clients Looking to Obtain a Patent

We work in prosecution, which means we help our clients understand what is patentable. We do this by finding out who our clients are, what their business is, who their competition is, what their opportunities are within their industry, and what their invention or idea is. Often clients come to us with an idea within which there may be multiple patentable inventions. In most cases, we suggest the first step be conducting a search to figure out what, if anything, is patentable; to see what the state of prior art looks like; to determine how broad or strong your registered patent would be if we went ahead and filed the patent application; along with multiple other benefits and strengthening pieces of information.

Not every patent, trademark, or copyright has the same value. Since the cost is so high to file and obtain a patent, there are a lot of factors that go into determining what the ultimate value is once a patent is obtained. For this reason and others, we depend heavily on a thorough initial search to figure out what the point of novelty in the invention is.

What is a point of novelty?

The point of novelty in an invention is that which sets apart the invention from all that is previously known; those elements or limitations in a patent claim that are novel, not conventional, not obvious, and thus protectable. The point of novelty is the key to what your patent protects.

Before proceeding with a patent application, we generally suggest starting off with a Point of Novelty (PON) search, analysis, and report. This report helps us to determine what, if anything, may be patentable, and whether the invention has already been disclosed in a patent or a patent application by someone else. The PON search also helps us in drafting the application and we believe it ultimately results in a stronger, more valuable patent application that will usually reduce the overall cost of obtaining the patent. This report ultimately helps us and the client make an informed decision as to whether the investment to proceed with the patent is a smart one.

Once we and the client decide patentable subject matter exists, the next step is deciding which type of patent application is most sensible. There are numerous types of patent applications including provisionals, non-provisionals, utilities, plants (which our firm does not handle given the necessary understanding of asexually reproduced plants), and designs.

If we do find relevant patent matter during our PON search, how we decide to proceed and how much to disclose depends on the invention and the product. Sometimes, a product has multiple inventions within it, so we might decide to file a single application that discloses all of the inventions within the product in the "kitchen sink" approach. With this approach, we may only claim one of the inventions in order to cut down on fees at the beginning, knowing that we're going to have to file subsequent applications based on that initial application in the future. We do this to lock in the earliest filing date for priority. Then, once we get the first allowance, we file an entirely separate application either as a "continuation" or a "continuation in part" which draws off of some other inventions from that initial filing. Generally, you'll get that second, third, or fourth allowance of an invention faster once an initial allowance is received for the first disclosed invention.

What is a Provisional Application for a Patent?

There are situations in which we suggest filing a provisional application as the best first step. The provisional application allows you to claim a date establishing disclosure as the original inventor of a product, but it **cannot** directly lead to a registered patent. It is a less expensive, less complicated application to file that discloses the invention and gives you a 12-month window within which to file for a non-provisional patent in the US. We often suggest a provisional application to clients who intend to disclose an invention in a public forum, such as a trade show, in the near future and we know there will be no time to draft a quality non-provisional patent application or conduct a proper Point of Novelty search.

In the case of a client who is still working on a product they know will change before being finalized, we may file multiple provisional applications over the period of product development to give them the most protection possible while they're still fine-tuning their invention. The goal is to include the disclosures in these provisionals in a single future non-provisional patent application that will hopefully lead to a registered patent.

What is a Non-Provisional Application?

A non-provisional patent is what most are familiar with when patents are referred to. These get examined, and when approved, become registered patents. While a provisional application has very few requirements for what is acceptable, a non-provisional has many formal guidelines and can get very complicated, but when prosecuted correctly, ideally leads to a registered patent.

Given all of the formalities and post-filing correspondence between the applicant and the USPTO, the patent process is generally much longer than most people realize. Most patent applications are initially rejected for substantive or procedural reasons. There are generally a few rounds of official communications with an examiner at the USPTO that may span several years. If handled properly the number of rounds and the negative effects of these official communications can be minimized. This, along with proper due diligence in the form of a quality prior art search before filing, make for a smoother application process from application through to registration.

What is a Design Patent Application?

Design patents cover the aesthetic design rather than the functionality of a product (i.e. what the product actually *looks* like). A design patent does not protect how that product actually works. This is an application we commonly use for our clients in the fashion and art industries, though it can be applied to otherwise patented inventions to cover the aesthetic aspects.

What Else is Important to Know About the Application Process?

Though not part of an application, we also work with our clients to clear their use of a technology known as the freedom to operate (FTO). While the applications discussed above are the offensive aspects of patent prosecution, from a defensive standpoint it is important to ensure that you are not infringing on another's patent in your mere use or marketing of an invention even if applying for a patent is not part of your plan. Conducting an FTO search and analysis is generally a big undertaking and quite expensive, but may be worth the cost when it results in avoiding what could have been a lawsuit for infringement.

Estimated Cost of the Patent Process

For the initial searches for a utility invention, cost can range between $1,800 and $4,000, depending on how deep and extensive the search. Upon deciding to proceed with a patent application, cost varies depending mostly on the type of application.

For a provisional application, fees will generally be between $4,000 and $8,000, depending upon complexity of the invention itself as this will determine the difficulty in drafting a quality specification for submission.

A non-provisional utility application will usually cost anywhere from $7,500 to $13,000, initially depending on the complexity of the invention. The main difference in the cost comes with the fees incurred after filing a non-provisional. Unlike a provisional which will not require much attention after filing, a non-provisional requires post-filing procedures, responses, actions, etc. and will therefore be at least an additional $7,800 once the application is filed.

For a design patent application, the cost is usually between $2,000 and $4,000 not including a draftsman's charges if the client is unable to provide proper drawings of the design. Depending on the detail and complexity of the design, we usually recommend hiring a draftsman since the USPTO requirements are specific and draftsmen are not only experienced in creating product drawings, but understand the nuances of the USPTO requirements for submitted drawings.

It is important to keep in mind that the above noted fees are all estimates and it is impossible to project a quote without understanding the scope or requirements for each individual client or invention. This is one of the reasons we always first speak to a client. Every client, every invention, and every business plan is unique and requires its own, specialized IP plan.

CHAPTER 4

WHAT IS A TRADEMARK?

Trademarks ultimately protect consumers. A trademark can be anything that denotes the source of a product or a service. When you see the Nike Swoosh, you know where that product is coming from. Whether it is on a shirt or a hat, you know that it is coming from Nike, and you know the quality to expect. Generally speaking, any symbol, word, logo, or color can be a trademark. Since a logo is a piece of artwork, it may also be possible to register a copyright for the artwork, but the trademark is the source identifier.

Trademark registration means that someone else cannot use that registered word, color, or symbol if there is a likelihood of confusion between the represented goods or services. Likelihood of confusion is the base standard used by the USPTO in examining a trademark application before most any other requirements for registration are even considered. The controlling standard for determining the likelihood of confusion is whether the purchasing public would mistakenly assume that the product or service offered by one specific entity, in fact, originates with, is sponsored by, or is in some way associated with the goods or services offered by another entity under another mark, or vice-versa.

The likelihood of confusion pitfall is one of the most important reasons why the first step with our trademark clients is a search. And why we say it can never be too early to speak with an attorney, but it can be too late. Before using a desired brand name or logo, we want our clients to know what already exists in the market and avoid confusion or potential infringement. The way to gain the best insight is with a thorough search looking at a similar name or logo registered or used in the marketplace that might create confusion.

The two most important factors that the USPTO uses to determine whether likelihood of confusion exists when an application is examined are the overall appearance and commercial impression of the mark and the goods or services that the mark is used in connection with. In other words, will the newcomer's mark likely confuse relevant purchasers and prospective purchasers? As such, minor changes like differences in spellings don't necessarily matter because it's more about the overall commercial impression.

Benefits and Limitations of Trademark Protection

The benefit of a trademark is that if you own the trademark for a specific brand for a certain type of good or service, you can (and it is in fact your duty to) keep others from using a similar name or brand that might cause consumer confusion. Trademarks are ultimately about protecting the consumer, so that the consumer is not confused as to the source of goods or services associated with a brand. As such, if someone infringes on your registered trademark, you may forbid them from selling or using that brand and can be awarded damages.

In the US, the only way to obtain a trademark registration is to submit proof of actual use of the applied for mark in the US in conjunction with the specified goods or services. These goods and services are listed in a manual and defined by International Classes (ICs)[4] which are largely organized by categories, subject matter, products, services, etc. that keep related items within the same IC. Once a trademark is obtained, registration covers and protects only the relevant goods and services.

What Can Be Protected by a Registered Trademark?

A trademark is any word, phrase, symbol, and/or design that identifies and distinguishes the

---

[4]https://idm-tmng.uspto.gov/id-master-list-public.html

source of the goods of one party from those of others. Some terms might make for weaker trademarks but can still be potentially trademarked. Terms that are the generic name of a product or service, such as "computer" for a computer, "lawyer" for lawyers' services, etc., are not protectable.

Services That Our Law Firm Provides to Clients Looking to Obtain a Trademark

We always hope that a client will come to us before they adopt a name or brand. Whether they do this or not, before filing a trademark application for a client we conduct a comprehensive search to assess whether we think the client might infringe on another's trademark if they adopt this trademark, whether we see other potential issues with using the trademark, if we believe we can obtain registration, and how strong that protection under the registration will be. With this information we can assist a client to make an informed decision of whether or not they should move forward with the desired name or brand.

It is not uncommon that a client comes to us years after they start using a name and have built a website, started putting up their signs, and designed product packaging. By the time they decide they want to trademark the brand and come to us, we conduct a search and find one or more issues. The choice between the monetary cost to rebrand or taking the risk of moving forward, knowing that at some point, they might be infringing on someone else's rights is a decision they have to make. Having conversations to rebrand or risk so late in the game turns my stomach because I know it could have been avoided.

Our firm's general policy is to conduct a search before filing a trademark application. Before we even do this, however, we strongly suggest that clients do some due diligence on their own to increase the likelihood that by the time they come to us for a search they have weeded out some potential conflicts.

Once we do conduct a search and the results are reviewed and discussed with the client and the decision is made to proceed, we go ahead with preparing a trademark application. We counsel the client on the best course of action regarding the wording and description of goods and services since, if done incorrectly, this can jeopardize a trademark application. We then prepare and file the application. Once it's filed, we monitor the application, handle correspondence with the Patent and Trademark Office, monitor and docket actions through to and after hopeful registration, and counsel our clients on how to use it.

After registration, we also offer and strongly encourage use of a watch service to clients that helps police intellectual property and provides information about potential infringements. Since it is an owner's responsibility to be aware of infringers, this makes it much easier. While the USPTO will usually reject a new application if found to be too similar to existing trademarks, they will not actively stop anyone from using and infringing on any trademark. Stopping the infringement is up to the owner. We help our clients come up with plans on how to protect and monitor their intellectual property and specifically, their trademarks.

The Cost of Filing a Trademark Application

For a trademark, our current fees start at between $1,725 and $2,000 for a comprehensive search plus preparing and filing a trademark application, along with monitoring of the application once filed. Of course, there are variances in the cost because it depends upon how many International Classes (ICs) are necessary. If the mark is to be used in relation to both a product and a service, it is going to be at least two ICs.

We also work with clients who file international trademarks, but here cost is impossible to estimate without knowing first in what specific countries the application will be filed and in what IC(s) the mark will be filed. In addition, for some countries, you can file directly through the USPTO whereas in other countries, a local firm needs to be attained for application and prosecution.

CHAPTER 5

WHAT IS A TRADE SECRET?

A trade secret is a business secret that adds value to that business and is its own area of intellectual property because it's intangible. At some point in time, prior to disclosure, most intellectual property is a trade secret. Most businesses have multiple trade secrets (ex. a customer list, a recipe, business practice or procedure, etc.).

How you keep a trade secret a secret is best done by having written contracts with your employees or independent contractors, who ensure that information is kept secret and only used for specific needs. If it happens to be a physical item, such as a written recipe, that trade secret also needs to be physically (i.e. locked in a safe) kept a secret.

A trade secret, once it gets out, is no longer a secret. Some of the most famous trade secrets are the formulas for Coca-Cola and KFC. Trade secret protection only protects you against those that you have a contract with to keep it a secret. If a third party comes up with it, it is no longer a secret. The only real way to protect the trade secret is by taking active steps to maintain it as a secret.

The Defend Trade Secrets Act (DTSA) of 2016 was signed into law on May 11, 2016. Now, misappropriation under the DTSA, in general, includes: without permission (A) obtaining a trade secret that was knowingly obtained through improper means or (B) disclosing or using a trade secret without knowing either (1) that it is a trade secret or (2) that it was obtained through improper means. The "improper means" include "theft, bribery, misrepresentation, breach or inducement of a breach of a duty to maintain secrecy or espionage through electronic or other means." However, misappropriation does not include "reverse engineering, independent derivation, or any other lawful means of acquisition."

How and When Does a Company Develop and Implement a Trade Secret Protection System?

You need to think about your business and what it creates. After that, you need to figure out what the process is that you need to develop to keep your creation a secret. Who needs to know about this secret? Whoever needs to know about it must sign an agreement to keep your secret a secret. If you're dealing with third parties or if you're a startup, you need to maintain this secret as a secret.

One of the questions you need to answer very early on, before filing a copyright or patent application in most cases, is whether your idea is better protected as a trade secret. When filing for a patent with the Patent and Trademark Office, you disclose your idea or invention in order to obtain a patent. Since the patent application becomes available to all upon publication, it teaches anyone who wants to know, how to use and make this invention. Similarly, if you file for a copyright, you must file a deposit copy of the work (software code). As both become publicly available information, by definition they are no longer (trade) secrets.

CHAPTER 6

DO I NEED A PATENT, COPYRIGHT, OR TRADEMARK?

In a perfect world, you would file for everything you think of or create. In reality, you need to do a cost-benefit analysis. Does it make sense to file for this? Will this be an asset for the business or is it a liability to continue to pay the fees and expenses of filing a trademark or a patent? All intellectual property is not created equal. If a patent would be very narrow and your competitors could get around it and create something nearly identical without infringing, we would likely try to dissuade you from filing for a patent.

The same goes for a trademark, depending upon what you're using. If we think the protection would be very narrow on a trademark, we might say not to file. We do our best to understand the factual and circumstantial issues, like what the client's needs are and why they want to file.

Before filing, one of the first steps is knowing what you have and how it works. See the flowchart below. We generally want to do due diligence both from a business perspective and a legal perspective. The client should generally be the one who is going to do the business's due diligence and then come to us. The client should become an expert in their product, service, and market if they are not already. We want to know where the product will be sold. Is it going to be sold online or at a larger big box retailer such as Walmart? Are the competitors' products at the same price point? Are there other similar items on the market? How are they selling? If there is no one else out there selling this product, then we generally tell our client to think about why no one else is selling it. Is there a real market for it or has no one come up with a cost-effective solution for which customers will be willing to pay? We combine the business due diligence with the legal due diligence to help the client figure out how best to move forward.

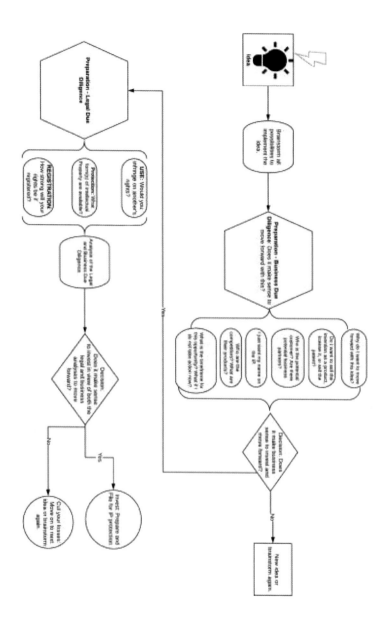

Idea

Brainstorm all possibilities to implement the idea.

Preparation - Business Due Diligence: Does it make sense to move forward with this?

- Why do I want to move forward with this idea?
- Do I want to sell the invention as a product, license it, or sell the patent?
- Who is the potential customer? Are there preferred business partners?
- I just want my name on the patent.
- Who are the competitors? What are their products?
- What is the business for this opportunity? What if I do not take action now?

Decision: Does it make business sense to invest and move forward?

No → New idea or brainstorm again.

Preparation - Legal Due Diligence

- USE: Would you infringe on another's rights?
- Protection: What form(s) of Intellectual Property are available?
- REGISTRATION: How strong will your rights be if registered?

Analysis of the Legal and Business Due Diligence

Decision: Does it make sense to invest in view of both the legal and business analysis to move forward?

No → Cull your forward: Move on to next idea or brainstorm again.

Yes → Invest: Prepare and File for IP protection.

Yes

What is the Right IP for Me?

Some products or businesses can be protected by multiple forms of intellectual property. Software code, for example, is copyrightable but it can also be kept and maintained as a trade secret, and the invention contained in the code may also be filed under a utility patent. Something like a graphical user interface could potentially be filed as a design patent and as copyright. Considering which form of IP is relevant to your business and taking advantage of all that are appropriate in a given situation will ultimately build the strongest IP portfolio and establish hard boundaries for a competitor to get around.

Features to Protect	Utility Patent	Design Patent	Trademark/ Service mark	Copyright	Trade Secret
Brands, Product Names, and Business Names			®		
Logos			®	©	
Slogans			®	©	
Two-Dimensional Designs		№		©	
Three-Dimensional Shapes (Appearance not Function)		№		©	
Creative, Artistic Works (writing, art, video, audio, graphic, website design)				©	
Software Source Code				©	√
Software Functionality, Web Apps, Business Methods	№				√
How your invention works (an improvement on a device or way of doing something)	№				√
How your invention looks (aesthetic or ornamental design, GUI)		№		©	
Formula, Recipe	№				√

® = Trademark or Servicemark
© =Copyright
№= Patent
√ = Trade Secret

63

We always try to figure out what form of IP our clients are going to get the most benefit from based on their business, the investment required and the protection the IP would provide them. In some cases we tell clients not to invest in a specific form of IP, meaning we turn down work for our firm, because they are better off putting funds toward research and development, getting the product to market sooner, advertising the product, etc. As with all steps in building a business, there should be a strategic approach to handling IP and our goal is to help you take the most efficient path to successfully protecting your assets.

General Misconceptions About Trademark, Patent, and Copyright Registration

One of the biggest misconceptions surrounding all forms of IP is the timeline of how fast you can get to registration. If a client has never filed for a trademark, patent, or copyright before, they often think it is a much simpler and quicker process than it is. Generally, the soonest you might receive either trademark or copyright registration is eight or nine months. Most of the time, it is going to be much longer, and patents are even longer than that. Your patent application might sit for two years before it is even examined.

The cost involved in registering IP is also often underestimated. Between legal expenses, official filing fees, and indirectly associated fees related to the products upon which the IP is based, the costs add up quickly.

Registering IP is often a lengthy process. It is an investment in both time and money even when done correctly. For this reason, we always stress that there should be a plan and goal in place before filing to register any form of IP.

Another misconception is that you must file and register your IP before you can use your IP. It is always wise to file before disclosing an invention or a work or revealing a brand name, slogan, or logo, but there is not a requirement that you must do these first. It is just good business practice to do these first, so you do not waive any rights. The ability to obtain a patent can be lost if you disclose the invention prior to filing a patent covering the invention. In most cases, it is more important to ensure that your use of IP will not infringe on another's rights.

What Information or Documentation is Helpful When Filing for a Trademark, Patent, or Copyright?

When discussing patents, we want to understand how you came up with your invention. What was the need that was unmet in the industry? We take the inventor back to the beginning, then work our way through to really understand what they're trying to accomplish. As such, accompanying documents such as an inventor's log, diary, or journal that has dates of invention, drawings, sketches, photos, etc., prior research conducted on the state of the art, information on competitors inventions, etc. are extremely helpful in establishing a starting point for evaluating patentability.

In terms of trademarks, we want to see: all versions of the logo, word, slogan, or branding; what the products or services are that they plan to use the brand in connection with; how this brand is going to be used and marketed; results of any searches the client has done; and where the client is selling/advertising or plans to sell/advertise the products or service. If the trademark is already in use, we want to see illustrations of how it is being used and know the dates the client started using the trademark.

For copyrights we want to see: the work; understand how the work was created; who are the author(s); what part of the work is original; what part of the work is based on prior work or someone else's work; if the work was published to the public; and what the plans are for the work.

In short, anything documented, planned, or related to IP is likely something we need to or want to know to best help our clients.

Criteria to Determine Whether to Proceed with a Trademark, Patent, or Copyright

Our first conversations with a client are meant to assess the needs of the client. What is the timeline for their project or business venture? Is there a certain business opportunity that they need to capture? Are we running against the clock because they already disclosed this invention? Have they done their due diligence? And further. We want to understand why the client believes they should file for their trademark, patent, or copyright. Only then do we look at the first functional IP step.

At this point, we discuss whether we should, and how to, proceed with a search for a trademark or a patent, or for copyrights, what material needs to be reviewed to determine the best approach for filing.

I'll reiterate this point (possibly several times in this book): At our firm we want to understand **why** a client wants to file for a patent, copyright, or trademark - that is, what the goal is in registering their IP. If money is the goal, we want the clients to ask themselves whether someone will pay for their product, patent, brand, etc. and who that person is. While this seems an obvious question and point, it can dramatically shift our and the client's strategy. The same is true for any reason a client may have for wanting to register IP. The better we understand why a client wants a registered patent, copyright, or trademark, the better we can formulate a solid plan for success.

CHAPTER 7

STEPS NEEDED TO PROTECT AN IDEA, INVENTION, OR CREATION

When you first come up with a new invention, innovation, or creation, you should have a non-disclosure agreement (NDA) or non-circumvent agreement with those privy to your disclosure. Not only will these agreements prevent others from potentially using your invention or filing for a patent and claiming it as their own, but a formal agreement, even with people you trust, can help avoid uncomfortable situations if a relationship takes an unexpected turn. A non-disclosure agreement is essential. Document everything. When did you conceive of this invention? When did you start creating the logo? Who was with you when you created the invention or designed the logo? What did each person contribute? Keep records of all dates as related to each developmental step along the way.

As I noted in the Chapter 5, you need to decide before filing a patent application if your idea is better protected as a trade secret. Since upon filing for a patent you disclose your idea or invention, generally the idea can no longer be claimed as a trade *secret*.

Once it is decided to proceed with a patent, a common first step is filing a provisional application. If you're about to go to a trade show or otherwise disclose your invention, filing a provisional application will ensure you claim a date prior to the public disclosure without which an invention would be precluded from obtaining a patent in the US and many other countries. Filing a provisional application before disclosure is also important for those who hope to license their invention to a larger company rather than selling the product themselves. Additionally, the provisional application will provide you with "perceived ownership" over the invention. This means that though the invention is not yet a registered patent, you will be seen as the owner of the patent if and when that does happen.

In terms of trademarks, if a client's mark has yet to be used in commerce, the best first step may be filing an "intent-to-use" (ITU) application. The concept is similar to a provisional patent application in that it establishes a claim of date of conception; even though the potential trademark is not in "use" yet, the idea is publicized and another entity would have had to start using or have filed for the trademark before that date. An ITU application is a good idea if you're going to disclose your brand name or your logo to a third party to prove your original creation and ownership.

Legal Due Diligence When Filing Trademark, Patent, Or Copyright

For both trademarks and patents, before filing an application, the first step is a search.

With a trademark search, we have two goals: One is to determine how we believe the US Patent and Trademark Office will respond, and based on that response, whether we are optimistic that the mark will register; The other goal is to figure out if we think the mark is clear for the client to use it or if it may infringe on another's rights.

Similarly, we can do that for patents, but the clearance search for a patent is a significantly more complex undertaking. Often with patents, we just do what we call a point of novelty search. This allows us to search through and find information about what other inventions or patents may be out there and whether we believe a patent can be obtained for the invention. The point of novelty search also provides insight into how broad the protection may be that we believe we can obtain. Depending on a client's plan and business model, we may advise them to forego the patent based on what the point of novelty search reveals.

In terms of copyright, a search is generally unnecessary so long as we are dealing with an original work from the client. We speak with the client to understand how the work was created, who created it, and who worked on it, to make sure that the client is the legal owner of the copyright in the work. At that point, we file the copyright application with the client either as owner and creator or based on the work being developed under work for hire by a contractor.

Once Legal Due Diligence is Done, What are the Next Steps?

Once the legal due diligence is done and after consulting with the client and deciding to proceed, the next step is to prepare for filing the correct application.

With patents we usually follow our initial assessment call with a more lengthy meeting to get more detail about the actual invention and what we should seek in filing (i.e. what part or parts of the invention should we claim?). Then, we come up with our strategy for drafting the application.

For trademarks, once a search comes up clear or the client decides after considering projected risks involved, they still want to proceed, we decide the best approach to filing. What is the most accurate description of goods and services associated with the mark? Should we file immediately for an ITU or wait until the mark is in use? It is a collaborative effort and information-based decision between our clients and our firm. We then prepare the application for submission and send it to our client for review and approval before finalizing.

Once a Trademark, Copyright, or Patent Application is Filed, What are the Next Steps?

As noted earlier in the book, registration is a process and it does take time. For a trademark application and prosecution that go smoothly, registration can take as little as nine months, but it can take up to two years or more.

A patent might not even be substantively reviewed until two years after filing. The back and forth between the USPTO and our office is known as prosecution. Some issues raised are minor and easy to address while others might be more difficult to overcome. In the legal due diligence we conduct prior to filing, we do our best to predict what will happen to assist the client to make an informed decision while considering additional costs and related risks.

A common misconception is that you need to wait until your intellectual property is registered before you can use it. That is not the case. In some cases, it might be a good idea, but generally the most important first step is a clearance search. A search should be conducted in order to best confirm that the IP landscape is clear for use of the product without worry of infringement on another's rights. As it pertains to trademarks, in the US a registration cannot even be obtained until the mark is used in commerce with the claimed goods and/or services. We recommend to our clients to start building their business right away rather than waiting until the IP is registered. Once your IP is registered, getting the product or the invention to market can take many different avenues. Are you going to make the product yourself or are you seeking a third party to license it or buy the patent from you? For a trademark, you need to provide the service or sell the goods under the trademark; in some way make it available to the public or intended consumer.

How Do I Protect My Intellectual Property from Being Infringed Upon in the Future?

Once a patent is filed, it is important to literally mark the product as "patent-pending" and state this when disclosing the invention. For trademarks, if the mark is in use but not registered, use a ™ symbol. Once it is registered, use the ® symbol. As soon as a client starts using their copyright, whether registered or not, we tell them to mark their creative work with the "copyright, *client name, year*, all rights reserved." This marking puts all others on notice of your rights and potentially can increase your damages if another infringes.

The final and most important point in preventing infringement is to always diligently police your own intellectual property. To aid in this for trademarks, we use and offer clients various watch services. For those that prefer to handle it on their own, there is always the option to simply set up Google alerts to see if another uses their mark.

For copyrights, there are companies that trawl the internet to find your photo or content on other sites. All of these services have different associated costs, depending upon what and where you're looking to protect.

If an infringement is suspected, we suggest the IP owner first contact an attorney to help determine if this is truly an infringement and if it is worth taking action.

Once I Have a Registered Trademark, Copyright, or Patent, Do I Ever Have to Revisit It?

Regarding copyrights, the laws were changed years ago, such that it is no longer necessary or possible to renew a copyright registration. Once the copyright is registered, there is nothing else to do, other than hope to make use of it and make money. If infringement is suspected, reach out to a qualified attorney to discuss whether to proceed with a cease and desist or take a different approach.

For trademarks and patents, there are maintenance fees and renewal fees, in order to maintain the life of the registrations. In addition to fees, to maintain a trademark registration, use of the brand on the goods or services it is registered for must be occasionally proven, or the registration may be subject to cancellation.

CHAPTER 8

COMMON MISTAKES THAT LEAD TO DENIAL OF IP REGISTRATION

There are some common mistakes that can cause a patent, trademark, or copyright to be denied. The most potentially critical step in avoiding some of these mistakes is to properly conduct thorough and careful legal due diligence before filing.

Your patent or trademark application is the initial offer in a negotiation with the USPTO. Once an application is submitted, it is the duty of the examiner (patents) or examining attorney (trademarks) assigned the application to inspect and determine whether registration is warranted and to try and find errors or inaccuracies in order to deny the registration. With each argument posed by the USPTO they chip away at the strength of protection for your IP. Anything you say in response can and will be used against you at a later date if and when you need to assert the claims related to your IP.

With copyrights, there is generally less back and forth and if an issue is found to warrant rejection of an application, it is usually just associated with a more objective reason such as the work being not original.

As it relates to IP, the list below is by no means exhaustive when it comes to mistakes that can be made and/or avoided, but legal due diligence and knowing what you are up against is the only way to start.

Trademark

For trademarks, the first common mistake we see made is choosing a descriptive word to brand a product or service. Obviously, the goal of a marketer or brand developer is to have a consumer look at the brand and know exactly what they're buying, unfortunately, as it pertains to trademarks, the more descriptive, the weaker it is. Even if approved by the USPTO, the resulting registration will be weak and, therefore, hard to enforce in instances of perceived infringement.

While the marketers push for descriptive, we as attorneys always prefer and suggest to our clients to opt for an arbitrary or fanciful name; one which no one else in the field is using, that has little, or preferably no, relevance to the marketed product or service.

Whether an attempt at flattery, trying to piggyback on another's success, or otherwise, a frequently made mistake when picking names, is using a competitor's name as "inspiration," and making a small change. This is rarely enough to register a trademark and using a mark too similar to a registered one may often be grounds for infringement. If you even think that your name is close to a competitor's, we generally suggest that you come up with something new.

When a client comes to us after having filed an application on their own there are two main issues that we see whether they come to us before or after receiving a rejection of the application. One of them is ownership. If ownership is incorrect in a trademark application, that trademark application is considered void, meaning that even if it goes through to registration, it is invalid. This can happen when the president or the CEO of a company files the trademark in his own name rather than in the entity's name, or files in the name of another company.

The other mistake often seen with self-filed applications is an inaccurate description of goods or services. Once an application is filed, and this goes for all intellectual property, what you can change after filing is quite limited. This means that when filing an application based on use, you must be accurate as to how the mark is being used. As such, when a client comes to us with a use-based application with an inaccurate description of the goods and/or services, we need to start from scratch with a new application.

With an intent to use application, anything can be listed, but in order to receive the registration, specimens proving the use must be submitted for at least one of the goods and services listed, with any other listed goods and services being deleted from the initially filed application.

Whether use-based or intent to use, the goods and services applied for can never be broadened, only limited, so it is always a good idea to think about what you are applying for and what your plans are for using the mark.

Patent

In terms of patents, one of the biggest mistakes we see is public disclosure of an invention or an attempt to sell before filing for the patent. In the US, if you wait longer than 12 months from when you first sell, use, or disclose an invention, you lose the right to obtain a patent. In many foreign countries, there is no grace period at all and once an invention is used or sold publicly, you cannot get a patent in that country. For this reason, it is best to file before you ever disclose the invention to anyone else.

Clients that come to us after already having filed an application, usually come with one of two issues: either the invention claimed is so narrow that it is of no real value, or there wasn't a search conducted and the invention is not patentable because there are other inventors who have disclosed something too similar. Neither of these problems are easy to fix – they may in fact be impossible to fix – and precisely why we stress the search and the importance of understanding what is out there.

Keeping good records for patents is a must because sometimes you have multiple inventors that work on a patent application and, as with trademarks, accurate inventorship and ownership is imperative. The inventors need to be listed correctly in a patent or it could potentially have implications down the road and even lead to a voiding of your patent.

Just like with a trademark, once you file a patent application, you're stuck with what you file. There are very limited ways that you can add to a patent application if aspects of the invention were not disclosed initially. Ensuring that the application is drafted correctly from the beginning is important. We always suggest including as many figures and flowcharts as possible because you might miss something in the literal description and as the old saying goes "a picture is worth a thousand words."

Copyright

In terms of a copyright, issues with work for hire and obtaining ownership over the copyright are probably one of the biggest mistakes we see clients make. Whoever is the actual owner of that work is considered the owner of the copyright unless there is an agreement that says otherwise. Having a work for hire agreement or another independent contractor agreement which includes in it that the copyright is being transferred upon creation is a good idea to ensure that you own the underlying copyright.

We see the ownership issue especially frequently with graphic designs. A freelancer or artist will create a logo for a client and if there wasn't a proper agreement, the client does not own the copyright on the logo, the artist does. If the client wants to make any changes to the work, they have to go through the designer to do it.

Having the proper agreements with third parties ensures that you own the intellectual property that is created. People think that they can use a non-disclosure agreement as a substitute for an independent contractor agreement or a work for hire agreement, but it cannot be done. A non-disclosure agreement has a specific use. It is usually to keep whatever you're disclosing to a third party a secret; It does not take the place of a work for hire or an independent contractor agreement and there should be proper documentation for that.

CHAPTER 9

WHAT SETS OUR FIRM APART FROM OTHERS IN THE HANDLING OF IP CASES?

We view our relationship with our clients as a partnership rather than a traditional counselor-client dynamic. That is, rather than providing only the necessary information and instructing the client, we prefer there be a dialogue as we believe this will add the most value to their business. Strong relationships (even business relationships) are built on trust and communication.

In following, there are situations in which we may recommend that a client does not file for a patent or trademark or take a certain course of action if we believe it's a smarter move for their business, though on our end it means we don't get to bill for more work. We want our clients to make an informed decision based on what we and they know collectively, so we always encourage open dialogue since we know this ultimately leads to a stronger relationship and more success for all parties involved.

We also have a less traditional approach to billing and cost as we prefer to work on a fixed fee basis when possible rather than charge per minute or hour of our time. Depending on the task, we will typically not charge clients for phone calls since we consider this to be an integral part of the established relationship. We want our clients to feel comfortable calling us and know they will not immediately be attached to a timer and charged for the minutes spent. In being a small business ourselves, we empathize with other businesses and love to see them grow and prosper.

What Common Denominator Do We See in Our Successful Clients?

What we see is that ideas are a dime a dozen, but successful clients, with or without patents, trademarks, or copyrights, take action and turn those ideas into inventions, products, services, brands, etc. They're committed to building their business, making efforts, and turning the product into a success.

Some clients get the IP protection, but after that, they take no steps. They're not getting it to the marketplace, so no one knows that their invention, product, or service even exists. Our most successful clients are our most proactive clients, both in business and in obtaining legal protection.

What Does Our Relationship with Our Clients Look Like?

The relationship depends upon the client and what their needs are. Sometimes, we get a one-off inventor or someone looking to do one trademark or copyright and we work on that single project with and for the client. Fortunately for us, many of our clients are lifers. These are individuals or businesses who we work with not only on, say, registering the trademark for their new brand, but maybe helping them build their entire IP portfolio around the plans for their business. We might work with our clients as they continue to come up with new products to trademark, patent, and/or copyright.

Whatever the basis for the initial contact, we don't like to look at anything as just a one-time transaction with clients. We always want our clients to feel comfortable to call us and let us know what is going on with their business. To encourage this, we use flat fees for most matters, so clients know every time they call us, it does not mean we're counting the minutes and charging them. I am very proud to say that we still work with many of the clients that I started with when I first opened the firm in 2009.

APPENDIX

Quick Guide to Selecting a Name for Your Business:

- Brainstorm potential names and list them in order of preference
- Remember that the more descriptive a name is for the goods or services you plan to sell, the more likely others will be using it and that, if registered, it will be a weaker trademark
- Do a web search for potential names. We suggest you conduct Google, Bing, Yahoo, Amazon, eBay, Yelp, Open Table, Resy and any other industry-specific searches on your own to assist in settling on your favorite name that you are relatively sure is not out there. Also, search for registered trademarks using the following:
  - TrademarkNow's Examatch: www.trademarknow.com/products/examatch;

- o USPTO's TESS: https://www.uspto.gov/trademarks-application-process/search-trademark-database;
- o WIPO-https://www3.wipo.int/branddb/en/; and
- o https://www.tmdn.org/tmview/welcome
- If you find anything similar, move on to your next option. Once you have exhausted all your efforts and are ready with a name, hire an attorney to conduct a Comprehensive Search.

INDEX

NOTES

Printed in Great Britain
by Amazon

70030754R00054